WHO AM I?

Who am I?

Titles in the series

Black-and-White (Panda)
Furry and Fluffy-tailed (Rabbit)
Long-necked and Lean   (Giraffe)
Winged and Wild (Golden Eagle)

I am black and white, big and bearlike.
I live in China.

WHO AM I?

By Moira Butterfield
Illustrated by Wayne Ford

Thameside Press

Distributed in the United States by
Smart Apple Media
1980 Lookout Drive
North Mankato, MN 56003

ISBN 1-930643-91-8

Library of Congress Control Number 2002 141344

Printed by South China Printing Co. Ltd., Hong Kong

Editor: Stephanie Bellwood
Designer: Helen James
Illustrator: Wayne Ford / Wildlife Art Agency
Consultant: Steve Pollock

I'm black and white from head to toe.
I'm furry, quiet, shy, and slow.
My favorite food is tall bamboo.
I hold it in my paws to chew.

Who am I?

Here is my eye.

I'm always looking for bamboo plants to eat. I find them growing in the forest where I live.

Other animals live here too. Can you see a monkey called a macaque and a deer called a sambar?

7

Here is my fur.

My fur is white
with black patches.
It is very thick
so it keeps me
warm and dry.

The mountains near
my home are cold
and snowy. I need
my warm coat when
I am in the mountains.

Here is my front paw.

I am very good
at holding things.
I can curl my front
paws around juicy
bamboo stems.

I use my sharp claws
to scrape up plants
and roots from the
ground. I like to
eat these too.

Here are my teeth.

They are big and
strong. I use them
for chewing and
grinding my food.
I eat all day long.

Sometimes, I bang
my teeth together
to make a chattering
noise. See if you
can do this too.

13

Here are my back legs,

Sometimes, I climb trees. I use my big back legs to push myself up. I am a very clumsy climber!

If there are wild dogs near, I might hide up a tree. Who is sharing the tree with me?

Here is my nose.

I can smell this fierce black bear nearby. He won't attack me because I am big and strong too.

Sometimes, I meet animals who are just like me. I can smell them before I see them.

Here is my sleeping place.

I like to take lots of naps. I make
a soft bed out of leaves and twigs.
If I am woken up, it makes me angry.

I open my mouth and...
growl!
Have you guessed who I am?

I am a panda.

Point to my...

round ears

black nose

front paws

20

back legs

sharp claws

white tummy

I am called
a giant panda.

Here are my babies.

They are called cubs.
When they are born,
they are tiny and pink.
Soon they grow
strong and furry.

My cubs love to play.
They have lots of fun
swinging in the trees
and hanging upside
down on branches.

Here is my home

It is a forest high on a mountainside.

24

Can you see me sleeping somewhere?
Look for two wild pigs, three deer called
sambars, a snow leopard, and a black bear.

Here is a map of the world.

I live in a small part of a big country called China. Where is it on the map?

Can you point to the place where you live?

China

Can you answer these questions about me?

What kind of plant
do I like to eat?

What color am I?

What is the weather
like where I live?

How do I know if there
is another panda nearby?

What are my
babies called?

Where do I live?

What do I like
to do all day?

Can you name any
other animals that live
in the forest with me?

Here are some words to learn about me.

bamboo A tall kind of grass. Bamboo is my favorite food. I eat it all day.

claws The long, sharp nails on my paws. I use them for scraping up roots and plants.

cub The name for a baby panda.

forest A place full of trees. I live in a forest where lots of bamboo grows.

furry Covered in thick, warm hairs. My body is furry all over.

grinding Crushing something into small pieces. I grind food with my strong teeth.

mountainside The steep sides of a high mountain. I live on a mountainside.

paws My furry feet and hands.

stem The long stalk of a plant. Bamboo has a hard, thin stem that I like to eat.

INDEX

babies 22–3, 30
bamboo 5, 7, 11, 30, 31
bears 17, 25
bed 18–19
chattering 13
China 26
claws 11, 30
climbing 15
color 5, 8–9
cubs 22–3, 30
deer 7, 25
dogs 15
eyes 6–7
food 5, 7, 11, 31
forest 7, 30

fur 5, 8–9, 31
grinding 13, 31
growling 19

home 9, 24–5
legs 14–15
macaque 7

map of world 26–7
monkey 7
mountains 9, 24, 31
nose 16–17
panda 20–1
paws 10–11, 31
pigs 25
questions 28–9
sambar 7, 25
sleeping 18–19
smell 17
snow leopard 25
teeth 12–13
world map 26–7